RICH KIDZ BIZ:

Business Basics

By

James Council, Jr.

Rich Kidz Biz: Business Basics

Copyright © 2020 by James Council, Jr.

ISBN (978-16364-9642-9)

Dedication & Acknowledgement

This book is dedicated to my sons Amari and Amir Council. I wrote this book to show kids that they could become business owners... at any age. Owning a business and being financially literate is a mindset. As parents, teachers, mentors, and simply people of influence... we tell children all the time that if they work hard, they can be anything in the world! So, why not teach them *how to be* financially competent and to also have an entrepreneurial mentality.

I grew up in a home where I knew nothing about finances. I didn't have my own bank account until I joined the U.S. Navy at the age of 18. I did not have the slightest idea what an investment was or the correlative phrases of assets and liabilities. "Rich Kidz Biz" was written to intentionally encourage kids to become money-smart, self-sufficient, and self-educated at an early age.

Additionally, this literary work will help parents understand that it is okay discuss finances with their children. We must obtain the mindset that as we learn, our children should also learn! As parents, we are their FIRST teachers, let's not omit financial literacy!

Special Acknowledgement to the incredible artist, Melisa Brown, for blessing me with her beautiful elephant artwork displayed on page 35 from her personal collection. To browse or purchase any of her additional artwork please contact her at:

Website: melisabrown.com

Facebook: facebook.com/iammelisabrown

Instagram: instagram.com/iammelisabrown

Table of Contents

Chapter 1: Asset... Huh

Andre woke up as his alarm went off and prepared himself for school as usual. After he brushed his teeth and washed his face, Andre walked to the dining room and greeted his mother, father and twin sister, Ashley, as he sat down to eat his breakfast. The night before, Andre saw a commercial for the new Falcon5000 drone, with voice-activated headset, 720p HD camera and 3.8 Ghz wireless controller. When he saw the new drone, he just had to have it. He was so excited, he dreamt about it.

While Andre ate his breakfast, he told his dad about the new Falcon5000. "Dad!" Andre said excitedly, "Have you seen the commercial for the new Falcon5000? I really want it... it's on sale right now for only $100! I've been doing really good in school, so do you think you and mom can reward me with it?" Andre just knew he had convinced his dad with his unrehearsed speech.

However, his Dad replied, "Son, if you really want it, you can use the money you've saved from your allowance to buy it." Andre jumped from the table and ran to his room to check his "cash stash" (i.e. one of his Nike shoe-boxes) that was inconspicuously hidden in the back of his closet.

He emptied his savings onto the floor and counted the money. To his surprise, he only had $42.53! Andre returned to the dining room, and matter-of-factly explained to his father that he needed an additional $57.47 so he could purchase the Falcon5000. Andre's dad looked at him lovingly, gave him a fist bump "Obama-style," and said... "Son, you are one of the brightest kids I know. If you really want that new drone; you have to figure out how

to create an *asset* with the money you

have." Then his dad left for work; Andre

sat at the table utterly confused. What did

his father mean by "create an *asset*?"

During his ride to school, Andre's mind

raced back and forth as he tried to

understand what his father meant. He had

heard the word *"asset"* before, but he didn't

completely understand or know the

meaning. Andre hated for anything to get

the best of him, so he Googled the meaning

of *"asset"* on his cell phone.

"An asset is anything of value or a resource of value that can be converted into cash."

His split-second search solved his frustration: as.set / ˈaset/ *noun* - anything of value or a resource of value that can be converted into cash. Individuals, companies, and governments own assets.

As Andre's mother dropped Andre and Ashley off to school, Andre saw his best friend Jordan. He kissed his mom goodbye in a hurry, and jogged towards Jordan. Andre enthusiastically told him about his latest technological pursuit of the Falcon5000 and the seemingly unfair suggestion of purchasing it "by himself!"

As they walked to class, Jordan asked Andre, "So have you come up with a plan to make the rest of the money you need?" Slightly annoyed, Andre replied… "No not yet, I didn't even know what *asset* meant, I had to look it up before I could even think of anything!" Then Andre quickly readjusted his attitude and confidently said, "But… before the end of the day I'm going to have a plan!"

At lunch Andre sat with Jordan contemplating "his $57.47 money plan."

A few seconds later his sister Ashley walked over and sat at the table accompanied by their friend Lisa. Ashley looked at her brother and asked, "Are you still thinking about how to make enough money to buy that stupid airplane you've been talking about all morning?" Andre sarcastically replied, "It's not an airplane it's a drone... There is a difference." "Whatever," Ashley retorted.

The lunch menu revealed that it was the infamously disgusting sloppy joe and tater tot day. Ashley hated it, so she pushed her lunch tray over to Andre and Jordan, it was one of their favorites.

Ashley held her stomach as she heard her stomach rumble, then she asked Andre for $2.00 to buy a snack from the vending machine. Andre reluctantly gave her $2.00. No sooner than Andre gave it to her, he regretted it; as he immediately realized he had dug himself into a deeper financial hole. He was left with only $40.47 to buy the Falcon5000.

Andre looked at Jordan and explained, "How can I make more money if I'm giving away what I have?" Jordan

shrugged his shoulders and replied, "If you
had your own vending machine you could
have just given Ash what she wanted.
Besides, she's your sister, it's not like you
are just giving your money to just anyone."
Andre sat up as he focused on what Jordan
had said. Then Andre shouted, "Jordan you
are a genius!" Jordan confusingly
responded, "Oooook Dre, I appreciate the
compliment...I guess."

While they finished up their lunch,
Andre told his friends and his sister to
meet him in the tree house after school. He
never explained why, but in an assured

tone he said, "This meeting will lead to the

opportunity of a lifetime!"

Chapter 2: Meeting of the Minds

After school, Andre met with everyone in the tree house to unveil his big plan. Dressed in blue jeans and sneakers, with a button-down shirt and tie... Andre explained his strategy to make some money. Andre asked "What makes more money from students in school than anything without much effort?" None of them answered, they just stared at Andre completely unimpressed! So, Andre answered his own question. "THE VENDING MACHINE," Andre yelled excitedly! "Dre, where are you going to get a $40 vending machine from?" Ash replied. "Andre focused his attention on Ashley and said, "Listen, dad said I need to find a way to make an asset so I could use it to make money. We can create an asset together. We can be the "vending machines..." if we invest our money and create our own candy shop!" Jordan appeared confused and asked, "Dre what do you mean by *invest*?" Andre adjusted his collar and in a self-assured tone he explained, "Lets become business partners, pool our money together, and start our own business. Together our money will grow faster in a shorter period of time than it does in our piggy banks. Our candy shop business is what the economic world calls an investment. The sooner we start, the sooner we can all buy our own Falcon5000s!!!"

Ashley and Lisa laughed at the ridiculousness they *heard* and seriously asked, "Why would we want to buy a stupid airplane with our money?" Andre scornfully replied, "I don't care what you buy, but if we work together as a team you can buy whatever you want! BUT Jordan and I are getting new drones!" Jordan high-fived Andre and confidently screeched, "I'm in, tell me where do we start?!" Andre looked at the girls and asked, "How about it? We can't do this without you." The girls cheerfully replied "Count us in too!" They solidified their agreement with fist bumps and enthusiastic chatter, Andre told everyone they'd meet again tomorrow after school to solidify their plans of launching their new venture. They came to the tree house as friends and parted ways as budding entrepreneurs.

Andre entered the house from the back door, and noticed his dad sitting in the den, in his favorite recliner. He said, "Hey dad!" His father responded, "Hey son, how was your day? Have you come up with a solution to get the money you need?" Andre replied, "My day has been… productive. I've got a masterplan in the works; we will chop it up after I do a little more research…" and Andre went to his bedroom. His dad smiled at him in admiration, he felt extremely proud of Andre, and uttered to himself, "Stuntin' like his daddy!"

That night, Andre spent several hours on his computer; he gathered as much information as he could on "how to start a business." He conducted his own virtual crash-course on entrepreneurship. Andre's parents went to check on him and noticed that he had fallen asleep; with his face pressed into his laptop's keyboard. His father picked him up like he had done when Andre was a baby and caringly laid him in his bed. As Andre's father covered him with his comforter, his mother kissed him goodnight.

Then, they walked into Ashley's room and

tucked her in for the night too.

Chapter 3: Money Plans & Candy Rain

Just like the previous day, Andre and his new business associates met in the treehouse after school. He was ecstatic to share the knowledge he had gleaned from his late-night internet research. Andre felt his appearance should match his position as the "Boss," so he wore a blue suit with a red tie to give his presentation to the team.

Andre cleared his throat, and allowed everyone to settle, then he confidently explained his findings. He felt the anticipation of his friends as he started speaking…

"Every new business needs to be securely funded as a "start-up" company. Since we are not old enough or qualified to obtain a traditional business loan from a bank… I suggest that we all contribute an equal amount of money to start our business. Everyone must make an investment of $30.00 into our start-up costs. We will purchase our inventory (the candy), equally disperse it and sell it. Our parents can take us to a store like Walmart or a warehouse so we can purchase our inventory in bulk. This way, we will get more bang for our buck! In other words, we will increase our profit margin automatically, because we are spending less in our overhead cost, thus increasing our profit!"

Ashley interjected and asked, "Dre, don't most of those stores require a membership card?" Andre replied, "Yes, that is why we will ask mom to allow us to use her membership for Lion's Club Warehouse... as long as we pay for it!" "Andre, are you sure mom is going to go along with this," Ashley asked? "Of course, she will," Andre said without hesitation!

Then Andre set up his dry erase board and placed it on a "makeshift" easel, the board had everyone's name and writing all over it. Dre had outlined everyone's various responsibilities and delegated their positions in the company. Andre explained the duties associated with each position. He started with his twin sister, Ashley. Dre focused his attention on her and said, "Ashley, you will be our CFO - the Chief Financial Officer. You're a natural wiz with numbers and math! You will keep an account of our financial cost and our company's earnings.

Anything that deals with money will go through you, Ashley." She beamed with pride as she happily accepted her position. Ashley had won several Mathematical Olympiads and Andre knew she would be the best person for this job. With a prideful smile on her face, Ashley said, "If it isn't numbers, it isn't me… Numbers rule the universe!"

Then Dre looked at Jordan and said, "Jordan, you will be our company's ODE - Organization and Development Executive. You're the most organized and disciplined kid we know!

This was an irrefutable fact, being that Jordan's father was a captain in the U.S. Navy... organization was a non-negotiable expectation in every aspect of his life. As our ODE, you will be responsible for planning and directing all aspects of our company's organizational and developmental functions. This position isn't for the faint-hearted. At times, you will have to organize and manage multiple tasks at any given moment, but I know you can handle it!" Jordan was definitely onboard with his new position; he had already taken down all the notes from the last meeting and organized them into a briefing sheet on his laptop. Andre was certain that he had chosen the right person for this job!

Last on the list of position delegation, was Lisa… Dre said, "Lisa you will be our company's DMRD - Director of Marketing Research & Development." Andre had known Lisa since they were in preschool, she was the most artistic kid in their class. The way Lisa created her art was more creative than anything Andre had ever seen. Her parents recognized her talent at a very young age, and they built Lisa an art

studio to help enhance her skills.

Art was Lisa's passion and she loved creating it. Dre continued his explanation, "As our Director of Marketing Research & Development, you will be in charge of creating our company's advertisements and finding ways to market our inventory creatively. Your creativity and marketing strategies will determine how successful our company will be. Our product presentation is profitably essential because marketing is the first thing that our potential customers will see!" Andre recognized Lisa's zeal for art, so he knew she would blossom in her position. Lisa gladly accepted the challenge without hesitation!

"WAIT!!!", Ashley blurted out. "Andre what is your JOB? You're not just going to let us do all the work." "Of course not.", Andre said. "I'm going to be the CEO - our company's Chief Executive Officer. I will assume the biggest challenge of them all, as the CEO I will have the most responsibilities out of everyone in our company." In an inquisitive tone Jordan asked, "Don't CEOs just sit in an office and tell everyone else what to do?" Dre quickly provided a rebuttal, "No, that is what you see on tv and in movies... CEOs don't just sit at a desk and spew out orders. As the CEO, I am responsible for making major corporate decisions, managing the day-to-day operations and the resources of our company. More importantly, I am the primary point of communication between the board of directors, which consists of the three of you and myself. I will be the face of our company and whether our company does good or bad... the public will always seek to address the CEO first! Typically, the CEO is ushered in by a voting process among the board and the shareholders. So, before I accept the position, I want to present the option of open nominations. Would any of you rather have the position of CEO?" Jordan, Ashley, and Lisa looked at each other simultaneously and replied, "We nominate YOU!" They smiled and laughed in agreement. Everyone knew Andre was a natural born leader. Andre was a team captain for the middle school basketball team, Youth Leader, and President of the Key Club. Andre was never afraid to speak his mind, take chances, or afraid of failure.

Chapter 4: Becoming an Expert

After everyone was assigned their new position and responsibilities, Andre encouraged everyone to research their new job titles, for the remaining time of their meeting. He wanted them to ponder over innovative ways each department could contribute to the company. By the time their meeting concluded, they wanted to have the name of the "Candy Shop" set in stone…

Jordan suggested they name it *Three Musketeers*, after his favorite chocolate bar. Andre immediately explained, "Jordan, that name can't be an option, it would be Copyright infringement, which is when someone uses the copyright-protected work of someone else, (a product, book, an article, a song, etc.), without permission! Besides, our team has four dynamic people and not three!"

Lisa interjected and addressed the team, "Why can't the name simply be *"The Candy Shop,"* I think an elaborate name is unnecessary! Especially, when we can have a name that tells our customers exactly what we are. I promise you guys, the artwork for the marketing pitch will be extraordinarily unforgettable." Andre looked over at Ashley and Jordan to gauge their reactions to Lisa's suggestion, and they unanimously agreed that *"The Candy Shop,"* was a perfect name. Alrighty then, "It's settled... "THE CANDY SHOP it is," said Andre.

The young entrepreneurs agreed to meet the next day, at the same place and time; they planned to discuss their research and plans with each other after completing their individual tasks for starting *"The Candy Shop."*

After everyone left, Andre knew he had to accomplish the important task of securing investors before their next meeting… in other words, it was time to ask his parents for assistance. So... Andre walked into the living room where his mother and father were watching a movie, and he nervously yet confidently gave his investment pitch.

"Excuse me mom and dad, sorry for interrupting your movie, but I need to run something by you all." His parents acknowledged him, and Andre proudly recited his "play by play" plan of creating an asset with his business partners, thus he wouldn't need the reward he requested from his dad previously. Andre informed his parents that "The Candy Shop," would be an extremely profitable asset and continued to vividly detail the plans...

"Right now, we are looking for investors to help with our start-up cost... Dad, this is where you and mom come into play," Andre explained. Andre's father and mother leaned forward, which was a direct indication that Dre had captured their interest. "Mom, Dad... investing in *The Candy Shop* will give you all the opportunity to be one of the few new investors for one of the most lucrative business ventures in our neighborhood. Think about it, what kid doesn't like candy?!? There is not a business like ours that is merely a 90-second walk from our customers front door." *The Candy Shop* will be one of the most profitable businesses in our area, possibly the world!

Before Andre could continue his impromptu pitch, his father stopped him because he knew Andre wasn't properly prepared to convince them to be investors.

"Son, before you approach any potential investors, you must prepare yourself. You don't have a presentation ready; you haven't worked out any financial numbers, and finances are a necessity when investors are involved. If your mother and I asked for your projected ROI, could you give it to us right now?" Andre shook his head in disappointment, and his dad continued… "When you and your business associates are completely ready, come back with a solid presentation that thoroughly outlines your business proposal. Then your mom and I, will consider the pros and cons of being one of

your selected investors."

Andre accepted his father's terms with great appreciation... but before he left Andre asked, "What is ROI?" Andre's father gladly explained, "ROI stands for "Return On Investment," which is a ratio between net profit and the cost of investment." Andre's mother interjected, "Dre along with the ROI also include *The Candy Shop's* sales forecast, net profit, company budget, fees for investors, and any additional information that may seem vital to us as potential investors."

Andre acknowledged his parents and thanked them for their advice. Before he left the living room, Andre shook his parents' hands and assured them that his team would be ready by tomorrow to make their proposal presentation.

Andre headed straight to Ashley's room; he felt an urgency to discuss *The Candy Shop's* numbers. Andre knocked on her door before entering… "Yes, my door is unlocked, open it." Andre opened the door and spoke in a rushed manner, "Ash, we must talk about our business's finances and an investment proposal, meet me in the study so we can work on it together… I think it's a lot to try and tackle alone."

Ashley immediately grabbed her

laptop and notes to meet Andre in their

study. The study was much like a library except its smaller. It had lots of books, magazines, dictionaries, encyclopedias, learning materials, computer access, and basically anything you needed to educate yourself and conduct research properly. As they sat down at their work desks, Andre explained the conversation that he had with their parents. "Ash, we need to have our investment proposal ready by tomorrow to get mom and dad on board." Ashley smiled and said, "Dre, I already completed the research regarding our finances. I've calculated the cost of our inventory from Lion Club's website.

Ashley, was already embodying a true CFO, she had a notebook with number graphs, profit equations, and an inventory list. Although Ashley's calculations were correct, it appeared unorganized and it looked like a foreign language to Andre. However, Ashley understood mathematical jargon as well Katherine Johnson (look her up if you don't know who she is).

Andre took a look at Ashley's handywork and suggested they call Jordan, their ODE (Organization and Development Executive); because he couldn't understand anything his sister had written down.

Fortunately, he knew Jordan would be able

to format everything in a manner that was

easy for everyone to understand.

Jordan answered Andre's call from his iPad... as soon as he answered Dre started explaining their company's urgent matter regarding their investment proposal. "Hey J, we need you to organize and format *The Candy Shop's* financial information, Ashley has already collected it." Jordan (as always) was already 10 steps ahead, he had built an excel spreadsheet to track supplies, quantities, cost, and product pricing; because of Jordan's efficiency, all they had to do was plug in numbers! They were about to start celebrating the completion of what they believed would be a long and tedious task, but Andre realized they still hadn't calculated a workable cost investment for potential investors. Additionally, their budget plan hadn't been solidified either. The three of them realized immediately, they had to become experts in every aspect of their business, and not just their assigned roles; entrepreneurship definitely requires teamwork and the *right* team!

Chapter 5: Conference Call

As Ashley flipped through her notes, she told Andre to add Lisa to their video chat. When Lisa answered, Ashley gave her a quick rundown of everything they'd already discussed. "Lisa, we called you because we need everyone's input for our investment proposal, and you're the DMRD (Director of Marketing Research & Development), so when one team member works, we collaborate as ONE team."

Ashley told the group that she had figured out a way to double their investment... if everyone (the 4 of them and

Ashley/Andre's parents) gave an initial

investment of $30 to purchase their

products, their budget would be $180.

"Listen up team, if we purchase 13 variety packs, we will have 636 items to sell. Our candy will be priced at $1 dollar, making our products cheaper and more appealing to our consumers. After selling everything for $1, we will have a profit return of $456, this is calculated like this: Investment cost = $30 X 6 Investors = $180. Then we SUBTRACT $180 (our initial investment) from our total sales of $636 = which leaves $456. When we divide $456 by 6 investors, the numbers prove everyone will collect a profit of $76, that is about 2.5 times greater than the initial $30 investment… Dre that would leave you more than enough to buy your drone…" Everyone's faces lit up with excitement!

Lisa excitedly projected her voice, "I have the perfect idea for our marketing plan. We should change our name to meet our company formula. Instead of the name being *The Candy Shop* it will be the *ONE4ONE Candy Shop*. Customers will pay $1 for any item… so the name makes perfect sense. The artwork is going to be lit! The number 4 in the middle would represent the four best friends who started the company together. "My head right now is bursting with new ideas; I have to write all of this down!"

Jordan chimed in, "There is still one very important factor we haven't settled yet... Where are we going to sell our candy? According to my research, there is a federal law in place that prohibits us from selling candy during school hours..." The "ONE4ONE" team looked at each and they didn't know what to say or do!

Chapter 6: Keeping it Legal

Andre acknowledged Jordan and stated, "You are right, but we have options. We will make the tree house our central location for the store. However, we will be mobile as well. Additionally, we will sell before and after school... This way we will not violate any federal laws. We will also make sales during various after school activities such as: sporting events, band practice, and club meetings. We will always have two *ONE4ONE* sale-representatives that are mobile, and the other two will be located at the tree house for store sales.

WEEKLY EMPLOYEE SCHEDULE

Date	Employee	Hours	Assignment	Lunch

We will develop a scheduled rotation to ensure everyone is treated fairly and this will help us to move our inventory efficiently." Everyone acknowledged it was an excellent plan to produce sales quickly! Andre instructed Jordan to create their rotation schedule on an excel document and he told Lisa to get started immediately on the artwork for their advertisements. Andre and Ashley worked on the presentation they'd be conducting for their parents as potential investors.

The ONE4ONE team ended their video call and went straight to work!

Jordan grabbed his laptop and started working on the rotational shift schedule. He also rechecked his data and compared the previous numbers he went over with Ashley to complete the inventory and financial spreadsheets. Lisa headed to her art studio to get to work on the flyers and posters ONE4ONE would use for advertising…

A few hours later, Andre realized that he'd gotten emails from Lisa and Jordan with their finished products to add within the presentation. Jordan's work on the financial data sheets and rotational shift schedule was immaculate. Jordan had also factored in 30-minute lunch breaks during the work day. Everything Jordan did was detailed and precise.

Ashley told Andre to pull up the artwork that Lisa emailed. When they opened the image, they couldn't help but smile with excitement over the logo and marketing flyers that Lisa created. It was SPECTACULAR to say the least! Every image had the ONE4ONE logo in the middle with big graffiti lettering.

Chapter 7: Branded Shirts

Andre and Ashley knew that they had chosen the right partners to help build their new business but they never expected what happened next. As Andre was about to close the email from Lisa, Ashley screamed "WAIT, we just got another email." When they opened the image, it was a t-shirt design that Lisa also created for all employees of the new *ONE4ONE Candy Shop*.

When Lisa's mom found out they wanted to start their own business, she told Lisa she would use her print shop to make their shirts… at no cost to them! It was her way of showing her support! This caused Ashley and Andre to feel even more excited and secure with their business and the investor presentation. Andre noticed that Ashley appeared exhausted, so he told her to go get some sleep and he would finish up the rest of the presentation.

The next morning everyone woke up ready to get their day started; they knew today would set the tone for the future of their new business. When Andre and Ashley arrived at school the next day, they noticed that Jordan was already there.

They told Jordan about the shirts Lisa's mom made. Andre created a thank-you card for Lisa's mom; he had Jordan and Ashley sign it. Just as Lisa and her mom pulled up, they all ran to the car to greet Lisa and her mom.

Lisa got out of the car with the box containing the team's new shirts. Their shirts were a different color shirt for every day of the week. The shirts not only had their new logo, but each of their names were embroidered on the front of their shirts. Everyone smiled from ear to ear as they admired their new gear. Andre gathered the team and presented Lisa's mom with a thank-you card and flowers to show their appreciation. Lisa's mom gave everyone a big hug and she expressed how proud she was of them. As they waved goodbye to Lisa's mom, Andre told everyone they would meet after school to go over the presentation for the prospective investors.

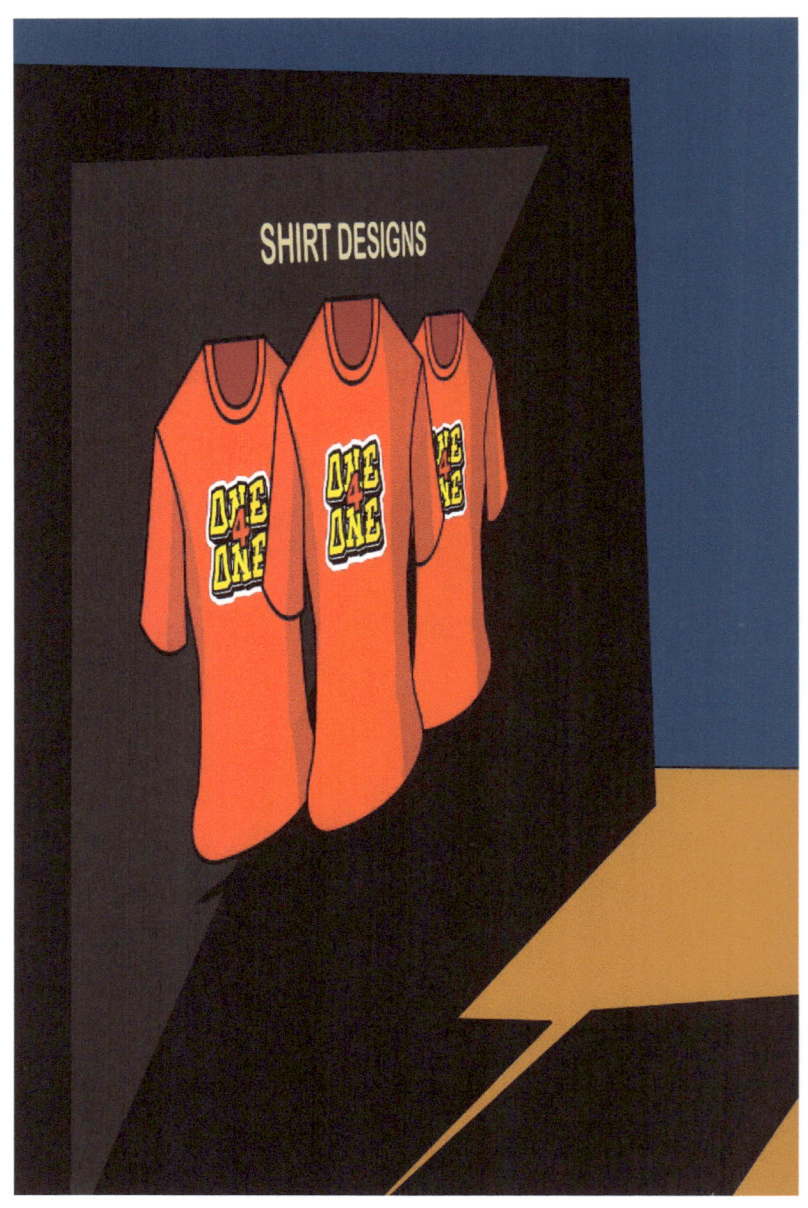

Chapter 8: Presentation for the Investors

Immediately after school, everyone met in the tree house to do a practice run of their investor presentation. Andre knew if they came unprepared [*this time*] there was no chance of his parents becoming investors. The meeting for their pitch was set to start at 5 p.m. in the living room of Andre and Ashley's home.

The team decided that they would arrive 30 minutes early to set up and conduct another quick run through of the presentation. They placed bottles of waters for their prospective clients on the table, along with two pens and two notepads so that they could take notes during the presentation. Their entire business plan relied on getting these two investors. The team went all in to make sure the presentation was flawless.

About five minutes before the meeting was scheduled to start, Andre and Ashley's parents arrived… and they sat in their designated seats in the living room. The *ONE4ONE* team was dressed in their customized team shirts made by Lisa's mom. Andre scanned the excited look on his team's faces and he could feel the anticipation from his parents... then he

confidently started the presentation.

"Before we start our presentation, we must thank each of you for your time and consideration! We do not take this opportunity lightly. My business partners and I are so happy to potentially have you all as investors. I'd like to introduce the team and their roles in our business, *ONE4ONE Candy Shop*. To my immediate right is Lisa, she is our company's Director of Marketing Research & Development... her creative artistry is A1 and bound to grab anyone's attention, next to her is Ashley, our company's Chief Financial Officer... She is a mathematical genius!

And standing beside Ashley is Jordan, he is our Organization & Development Executive - he is the brains behind our day to day operations. Finally, "I am our company's Chief Executive Officer, I love to lead by example with my actions and not just my words! With that being said, are there any questions before I proceed?" Andre's parents smiled at him, and shook their head in agreement for him to move forward...

Andre moved right into the presentation, he provided the financial breakdown of their company that included

ONE4ONE's ROI, marketing strategies, finances, inventory, and everything the team had discussed. As he went through the presentation and answered questions, it was impossible for him to gauge whether he had convinced the potential investors to take the plunge with them! Andre simply ensured that he provided a well-thought out business plan that would exponentially increase the probability of his parents saying, "YES to Invest!"

After Andre's closing remarks, his parents asked to give them a few moments while they discussed a few things. The team went outside near the treehouse and awaited the decision from their potential investors. They all felt anxious. Andre paced back and forth, as he replayed the presentation in his head from start to finish. He asked his sister and his friends, "How'd I do... tell me the honest truth!" Everyone assured him that he had done an incredible job.

After about five minutes, but it seemed more like five hours, Andre's father told them to meet him and his mother in the living room. Andre's father calmly said, "We've made our decision...

and we were very impressed with

ONE4ONE's business plan and

presentation. You all forgot one thing!" The

team's hearts sank to their stomachs!

"Don't be upset with yourselves, you all

just forgot to calculate fuel for travel

expenses to and from Lion's Club to

purchase your inventory. We are not

holding this against you all. Just remember

to include EVERY expense; in any

business... mistakes are inevitable,

especially with first-time entrepreneurs!

However, what matters most, is that you

learn from these mistakes."

The *ONE4ONE* team was certain

that they had lost their prospective

investors. Andre and Ashley's mothers

chimed in, "Don't look so disappointed, it

was an honest mistake and all you have to

do is go back and figure out the numbers

for travel expenses. After you figure those

numbers out, bring them back within the

next hour and if all your calculations come

back accurately... We will cover all travel

expenses and become investors. The

ONE4ONE team agreed to the terms and

went to the study to figure out the travel

expenses.

Jordan looked up the distance for the mileage from Andre and Ashley's house to Lion's Club, which was approximately five-point-five miles away. This would be 11-miles round trip. Lisa and Ashley, looked up the different gas stations in the area to locate the station with the cheapest gas prices. They found one that was less than a mile away from the home and the gas was only $2 per gallon. Andre quickly researched the fuel efficiency for his mother's car, which was 20 miles per gallon. Ashley told the team, "In order to calculate the cost for travel expenses, we must take the total mileage of the trip (11 miles) and divide it by the miles per gallon (20 mpg) of their mother's car. Then, multiply that figure (0.55) by the current price of gas ($2.00) and the result is the cost of gas for the trip = $1.10. Everyone ran through the numbers over and over again.

After everyone kept getting the same numbers, they were confident that they would be able to present this to their new investors. Andre presented the team's numbers and calculations for travel expenses. His father and mother wrote in the notebooks they were provided and double checked the team's calculations. Andre's dad looked at his mother and nodded his head in agreement. Then Andre's dad stood up and said, "Your mom and I would love to be the initial investors of *the ONE4ONE Candy Shop*." Andre's parents shook all of their hands as a symbol of agreement. Everyone clapped and celebrated the new partnership that they would explore together.

Chapter 9: Inventory Run

The next morning, Andre and Ashley rode with their parents to Lion's Club to pick up the items from their inventory list. Lisa and Jordan hit up schools, local businesses, and homes in the neighborhood to hand out their advertisements and post flyers for the grand opening of *ONE4ONE Candy Shop*.

After leaving Lion's Club, Andre and Ashley met with Jordan and Lisa in the treehouse to go over inventory and discuss their marketing efforts for the grand opening. Lisa had created a Facebook page for *ONE4ONE Candy Shop*, she posted information about the grand opening so they could reach a larger audience beyond their face-to-face interactions. This was an amazing idea because they also could list their inventory, bio, business hours, location, photos, provide live updates, and allow people to see their company slogan. Lisa was killing the marketing scheme with the help of Jordan right by her side.

The team decided that the grand opening would be on Saturday, because all the kids would be out of school. The neighborhood would be bustling with kids playing, or in other words *ONE4ONE's* potential customers! The mobile team would visit a few sporting events around town and use their bikes to transport products. Jordan brought an idea to the table that he believed would help move orders faster… he suggested, "Let's take pre-orders using our *ONE4ONE* Facebook page. This will help generate buzz and build momentum for the official opening on Saturday!" Andre and the rest of the team thought it was a fantastic idea. Jordan and Lisa added the announcement for pre-sales right away; while Andre and Ashley continued dividing the inventory for store

sales, preorder sales, and mobile sales.

Chapter 10: Go Time

The next morning, which was the day before their grand opening… the *ONE4ONE* team wore their business shirts to school [it was a marketing ploy]. Earlier that week, Andre was able to convince Principal Smith to allow them to post and pass out flyers for their grand opening at school. At the end of the school day, the ONE4ONE team met to go over last-minute plans for the grand opening. To their surprise, they had already secured 50 pre-orders for the Grand Opening! The team

knew that they were moving in the right

direction.

The morning of *ONE4ONE's* grand opening, everyone's parents showed up in support of their new business *and* they each purchased $10 worth of candy! Now, that is the kind of support you need as a budding business! After the "Ribbon-Cutting Ceremony," the team got straight to work. Andre and Lisa spearheaded the mobile sales, while Ashley and Jordan ran the *ONE4ONE Candy Shop* at the treehouse. Both teams filled the preorders first because they wanted to make sure those customers were recognized and appreciated for their "blind-faith support."

Business was booming to say the least! Small kids, pre-teens, teens and even some adults came to purchase from the *ONE4ONE Candy Shop*. They received several compliments regarding their customer service and affordable price, some customers even left raving reviews on their Facebook page. As *ONE4ONE's* mobile team completed their sales... they also had numerous people tell them how much they appreciated the convenience of their orders being delivered directly to them! *ONE4ONE's* Grand Opening was more successful than they imagined!

Chapter 11: Mission Accomplished

The *ONE4ONE* team worked

vigorously through the weekend, and they

continued selling throughout the week. In

just seven days the team had sold all of

their candy. Their excitement was

uncontainable! Their work ethic,

discipline, teamwork, fearlessness and

dedication to achieve a goal together had

paid off in a major way. The team

calculated their earnings of $636 and after

subtracting the initial investment owed to

all six investors of $180 ($30 each) leaving

them with $456. We are getting a Return

on Investment (ROI) of 153%. ROI reveals how much profit our money has earned. When we assess the ROI, we calculate it dividing the net profit by the cost of investment and then multiple by 100 to get the percentage, mathematically the equation looks like this:

ROI = N / C x 100

- **N = net profit from investment ($76)**
- **C = cost of investment ($30)**

ROI = $76 / $30 x 100 = 153.333%

The *ONE4ONE* team had more than doubled their initial investment within one week of opening their candy shop. And to think, it all started with Andre wanting to purchase the new Falcon5000 drone and his father challenging him to find a way to purchase it even though he didn't have enough money to do so.

Andre sat in the treehouse admiring the $106 he held in his hands ($30 initial investment + $76 profit), it was more than enough to purchase the drone he wanted. Lisa asked Andre "So, are you excited about being able to buy your new drone?" Andre replied, "I don't know." Ashley and Jordan confusedly asked, "What do you mean you don't know?"

Andre paused for a few minutes and said, "Right now we have two choices. One, we can leave with the money we have made and go purchase whatever we want right now and be satisfied momentarily until we want something new. ORRRRR TWO, we can use the money we made right now to reinvest back into our *ONE4ONE Candy Shop* that we built together and make even more money than before. Our customers are already waiting to purchase from us again! *ONE4ONE Candy Shop* just might be bigger than we thought... Whatever we decide, we will do so as a team." Andre looked around the room and everyone shook their heads in agreement. Finally, he asked "SO, WHAT ARE WE GOING TO DO… One time come-up or ensure a residual return?"

Entrepreneurship Terminology

Asset- a resource with economic value that an individual, corporation, or country owns or controls with the expectation that it will provide a future benefit.

Business-a company or other group that buys and sells goods or services in order to make money.

Capital-is a term for financial assets, such as funds held in deposit accounts and/or funds obtained from special financing sources.

Cash Flow- the total amount of money being transferred into and out of a business, especially as affecting liquidity.

Credit-the right to buy things at the present time and not pay until later. Having credit often depends on one's reputation for paying one's debt.

Debt-something owed to another person

Equity-the net worth of a business or property; total value of assets minus outstanding liabilities.

Expenditures-something which is paid out or spent.

Fungibility-is the ability of a good or asset to be interchanged with other individual goods or assets of the same type.

Gross Profit- is the profit a company makes after deducting the costs associated with making and selling its products, or the costs associated with providing its services.

Gross Revenue-also known as gross income, is the sum of all money generated by a business, without taking into account any part of that total that has been or will be used for expenses.

Income-the money received for work or from property that is owned.

Interest-is the charge for the privilege of borrowing money.

Inventory-the goods or materials on such a list.

Invest- to put into use for the purpose of making money.

Investment- something into which money, time, or effort is invested.

Investor-a person or company that invests or puts money into use for the purpose of making more money.

Liability-financial obligation; debts.

Liquid- in the form of money, rather than investments or property or able to be changed into money easily: *liquid assets*

Net Worth-is the value the assets a person or corporation owns, minus the liabilities they owe.

Net Profit- the actual profit after working expenses not included in the calculation of gross profit have been paid.

Property- all of one's possessions taken as a whole, or a part of those possessions.

Portfolio-the investments or securities owned by a person or company.

Residual Return- Return independent of the benchmark. The residual return is the return relative to beta times the benchmark return. To be exact, an asset's residual return equals its excess return minus beta times the benchmark excess return.

Resource- a stock or supply of money, materials, staff, and other assets that can be drawn on by a person or organization in order to function effectively.

Return on Investment (ROI)-measures the gain or loss generated on an investment relative to the amount of money invested.

Return on Revenue (ROR)-is a measure of company profitability based on the amount of revenue generated.
Security-is a fungible, negotiable financial instrument that holds some type of monetary value.

80/20 Rule-also known as the Pareto Principle, is an aphorism which asserts that 80% of outcomes (or outputs) result from 20% of all causes (or inputs) for any given event. In business, a goal of the 80-20 rule is to identify inputs that are potentially the most productive and make them the priority.

About the Author

James Council Jr. is a father of two boys Amari and Amir. He graduated from Woodland High School in Dorchester, SC and joined the military in 2004 at the age of 18. He currently serves in the United States Navy as a Chief Cryptologic Technician Technical onboard the USS Iwo Jima (LHD 7).

During his 16 years in the Navy he has completed 3 deployments while serving onboard the USS Oscar Austin (DDG 79), USS America (LHA 6), SPAWAR Space Field Activity (SSFA), COMUSNAVCENT Manama, Bahrain and Information Training Site Hawaii (IWTS Hawaii). While on active duty he completed his degree in Information Technology/Networking and is currently working a second degree in Financial Management.

While writing this book, James also started a real estate business group the Woodland Palmetto Property Group with three of his best friends to put his knowledge into action.

James' hobbies are reading, sports, writing, and learning ways to build passive income. James plans to continue his journey of authorship because he is passionate about educating others on the importance of financial literacy. Entrepreneurship doesn't have an age requirement; it simply requires time and strategic investment.

Printed in the USA
CPSIA information can be obtained
at www.ICGtesting.com
LVHW070927210524
780921LV00001B/2